I CAN ABOUT ANYTHING!

Mary Terese Donze, A.S.C.

"Unless you...
become like little children...."
Matthew 18:3

LIGUORI
PUBLICATIONS

One Liguori Drive
Liguori, MO 63057-9999
(314) 464-2500

Imprimi Potest:
James Shea, C.SS.R.
Provincial, St. Louis Province
The Redemptorists

Imprimatur:
+ Edward J. O'Donnell, D.D.
Auxiliary Bishop, Archdiocese of St. Louis

Printed in the United States of America
96 97 98 99 00   6 5 4 3 2

Cover and interior art by Bartholomew

To Jesus Christ—

Son of God, Son of Mary—

who once upon a time

was six.

CONTENTS

INTRODUCTION

Across the fields of yesterday,
there sometimes comes to me
a little child just back from play,
the child I used to be.

Thomas S. Jones, Jr.

The prayers in this booklet are intended primarily for the small child who is not yet able to read. The parent, grandparent, or other interested adult might read the prayers slowly in short thought-units and have the child repeat them. This will allow the child to make the prayer his or her own. Avoid reading the entire prayer to the child as if it were your prayer or even a prayer from a book. As much as possible, make it seem a loving emanation from the child's own heart. Later, when the child learns to read, he or she can use the book independently.

The word *mommy* is used in the prayers to refer to the child's mother. If the child calls his or her mother other than mommy, make the adaption when reading aloud to the child. Do the same with the word *daddy*. Also, if there is only one parent in the home, change the prayer to fit the situation. Otherwise, as much as possible, keep the text as it is.

The he-or-she form of usage has been avoided throughout the text as being awkward. Wherever the pronoun *he* or *she* occurs, simply substitute the appropriate form.

The prayer titled "My Prayer to Jesus in My Heart Room" is the only one of its kind and is the child's introduction to contemplative prayer. It is also the only prayer in which the adult gives directions to the child. Read the directions in a quiet, reverent voice—but without dramatics—allowing the child a time of quiet in which to speak in his heart to Jesus. *

Here are some further suggestions:

- Familiarize yourself beforehand with the prayer you intend to read that day, and take a few moments to dwell on it in the presence of God before beginning the prayer with the child.
- To set the atmosphere for each prayer, talk to the child briefly about the person or situation on which the prayer focuses.
- Use the prayers frequently with the child so that, for example, when a siren sounds or an airplane goes by or the child sits down to eat, she will remember the prayers and instinctively respond to the situation with a prayerful thought for the persons or things involved.
- Pray frequently for the child. Jesus, who loved little children with a special affection, is sure to bless your efforts to draw small Christians to his heart.

* (For similar contemplative prayers for children, see *In My Heart Room, Book One* and *In My Heart Room, Book Two* by the same author, also published by Liguori Publications.)

I CAN PRAY EVERY DAY!

My Prayer When I Get Out of Bed in the Morning

JESUS, thank you for this new day. I love you, and I will try to do everything I do today for you, Jesus. When I play and when I eat and when I just walk around and don't do anything special, I will think: *This is all for Jesus.* Bless me, Jesus. Stay with me, holy Mother Mary and all you good angels. Amen.

My Shower Prayer

JESUS, it is time for me to take a shower. I like taking a shower. I like the way the water runs down all over me. I like the way it washes me clean and makes me feel like new. Thank you for water and how there is enough of it to go around for everybody to have a shower. Amen.

My Prayer Before I Go Out to Play

JESUS, I am going out to play. Watch over me and the kids I play with so we have fun and don't get hurt. And if there is a new kid around or a kid that doesn't know how to play the game, show me how to be nice to (him, her). Help me remember to come home when I'm supposed to. Amen.

My Prayer Before Meals

JESUS, bless all the things we are going to eat. Bless Mommy for getting them ready for us. Bless the people who grew our food or made it and brought it to the store where we could buy it. Bless the people at the store who put the food into bags so we can carry it home and not drop it. Bless me, too, Jesus, and the children all over the world so we always have enough to eat. Amen.

My Prayer After Meals

JESUS, thank you
for the good (breakfast,
lunch, dinner). Thank
you, too, for how you
colored the things we
eat. I like the way they
are red and yellow
and all kinds of colors.
I am glad you did not
let them all be brown,
like prunes, maybe.
Thank you, too, for
how we sit at the table
and talk and laugh
and make it fun
to eat together.
Amen.

My Prayer Before I Go to Bed

JESUS, it is time for me to go to bed. Thank you for taking care of me all day. I am sorry if maybe sometimes I did things Mommy or Daddy told me not to do today. Help me do better tomorrow. I love you, Jesus. Bless Mommy and Daddy and all of us. Holy Virgin Mary and all you angels that belong to Jesus, watch over me when I sleep. Amen.

I CAN PRAY ON SPECIAL DAYS!

My Prayer on My Birthday

JESUS, today is my birthday. I am _____ years old. It is fun to have a birthday because sometimes you get presents or your mommy or somebody else in your family makes you a cake with candles on it or maybe somebody just hugs you real tight and says, "Happy Birthday! I love you!" That's the best of all. I like having a birthday. Thank you, Jesus, for how everybody gets a birthday. Amen.

My Prayer on Valentine Day

JESUS, today is Valentine Day. Kids and other people buy valentines with hearts on them, or they draw some hearts on paper and color them red. Then they give the valentines to their special friends. It's like saying, "You are my valentine. I give you my heart because I love you." You are my special friend, Jesus. You are my best valentine. I give you my heart. I love you, Jesus. Amen.

My Easter Prayer

JESUS, one time you died on the cross, and all the people who loved you were very sad. Then, after three days went by, you came alive again. You stood right up and walked around and surprised everybody and made them happy that you were alive again. That is why we have Easter. It is your special day. On Easter Sunday the people in church sing "ALLELUIA!" That means PRAISE THE LORD! I say ALLELUIA! to you, too, Jesus. Thank you for Easter. Amen.

My Prayer About Hunting Easter Eggs

JESUS, today is Easter. I am going to hunt for some Easter eggs. I like Easter eggs. I like their pretty colors. I like to eat them, too, with a little bit of salt on them. Jesus, thank you for Easter eggs. I hope all the kids find some.
Amen.

My Prayer on Thanksgiving Day

JESUS, today is Thanksgiving. Most people don't have to go to work or to school. We can stay home and just have fun, or we can go to visit somebody. We have Thanksgiving Day to remind us to thank you for all the good things you give us. I thank you today. Help me remember to thank you at other times, too. You are a very good God. Thank you for everything. Amen.

My Christmas Prayer

HAPPY BIRTHDAY, JESUS. Thank you for coming from heaven to be with us. I think it was not easy for you to leave all your nice things in heaven and become a little baby sleeping on straw in an old stable. But it was good that you did, because if you had been born in a fine house and looked rich and important, a lot of people would be afraid to talk to you or go into your house. But nobody is afraid of a baby. Nobody is scared to visit an old stable. I love you, Jesus, and I like how you love me, too. Thank you for making Christmas happen for all of us. Amen.

I CAN PRAY FOR MY FAMILY!

My Prayer for My Mommy

JESUS, thank you for my mommy. I love her very much. I think she is the best mommy in the whole world. She combs my hair and ties my shoelaces and gives me cookies and milk and does ever so many things for me. She loves me a lot. Sometimes, though, when I do things she tells me not to do, she stops smiling, and I think she doesn't love me anymore. But she does. Only she doesn't want me to do bad things. She wants me to grow up to be a good (girl, boy). Bless my mommy, Jesus. Amen.

19

My Prayer for My Daddy

JESUS, when you were a little boy, Saint Joseph took care of you the same way my daddy takes care of me. Saint Joseph had to work so he could buy you new shoes and things to eat and maybe something for fun once in a while. My daddy has to work so he can take care of me, too. Jesus, I wish you would bless my daddy for all the things he does for me. I love my daddy. I like it when he plays with me and we have fun together. Someday I want to be as big and as smart and as good as my daddy. Amen.

My Prayer for Grandma

JESUS, thank you for Grandma. She is very good to me. I like to visit her and walk around in her house and see all the things she's got. Sometimes Grandma lets me do things for her, too. And if she goes to the store or to church, she takes me with her. We like each other a lot, me and Grandma. I ask you to bless Grandma, Jesus. Amen.

My Prayer for Grandpa

JESUS, thank you for Grandpa. I think he is the best grandpa ever. He tells me stories about when he was little and all the things he did. He tells me jokes, too, and we laugh together. I like to do things with Grandpa because we are good friends. Jesus, bless Grandpa and all the other kids' grandpas, too. Amen.

My Prayer for Our New Baby

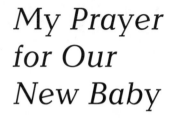

JESUS, we have a new baby at our house. *It's a baby girl. Her name is (baby's name). She is not very big and doesn't have much hair. Sometimes she cries, but mostly she doesn't. She sleeps a lot, too. I am glad we have a baby in our house because when she gets bigger, we can play together. Jesus, I wish you would bless our new baby and make her grow fast. Bless Mommy and Daddy, too, because they have to take care of the baby, and babies are a lot of work. I am going to help take care of our new baby, too. Amen.

*Substitute the appropriate form.

23

My Prayer About Our House

JESUS, we have a nice house. Everyone in our family tries to keep our house clean and pretty. If any of us—like maybe me—breaks something or spills some soda or milk or something else on the carpet, don't let us just walk away and not say anything about it like we don't care. Jesus, bless our house and all of us who live in it. Amen.

My Prayer About Our Car

JESUS, we have a car. Sometimes Mommy and Daddy use it to go to work. We all go to church in our car and to the store and to other places, too. A lot of people besides us have cars. Some people drive their cars very fast. If the cars bump into one another, somebody could get hurt. Jesus, bless my family and all the other people and make them drive safely so our cars don't bump into each other. Amen.

My Prayer for When My Pet Needs a Shot

JESUS, my (dog, cat, or other pet) has to get a shot today. (Pet's name) does not like to get shots. I think he* is afraid. Don't let him be too much afraid. Sometimes I am afraid to get shots, too. But I know you are in my heart, Jesus. You watch over me when I am afraid. I know you will watch over my pet, too. I love (pet's name), and I don't want him to get hurt. Thank you, Jesus, for making pets for us kids. Amen.

* Substitute appropriate form.

My Prayer for a Sick Friend

JESUS,_____
is my friend. She* is sick. I
want her to stop being
sick so we can go outside
and play again. Maybe I
could draw her a funny
picture to make her laugh.
Or I could make a pretty
picture, too, maybe some
flowers. Jesus, you used to
make a lot of sick people
get well. I wish you would
make _____ get well
again. Amen.

*Substitute appropriate form.

26

My Prayer When I Hear an Airplane

JESUS, I hear an airplane. I know it is full of people. I can't see any of them, but I know they are there. All of them are going someplace. Maybe there are some kids like me in the airplane. I don't know their names, but I pray for all of them. Bless them, Jesus, and make the airplane get down all right so everybody gets where they are going. And don't let them lose their bags with all their stuff inside. Amen.

My Prayer When I Hear a Fire Engine

JESUS, I hear a fire engine. There's a fire someplace. Maybe somebody's house is burning! Make the cars on the street get out of the way so the fire engine can get to the fire in a hurry. And don't let anybody be hurt. I pray for the firefighters, too, so they can put out the fire and not get burned or have to breathe a lot of hot smoke. And if it is somebody's house that is burning, help the people find a place to go until they get another house. Amen.

My Prayer When
I Hear an Ambulance

JESUS, somebody is sick or hurt and has to go to the hospital. I can tell because I hear the ambulance siren. Help the ambulance driver get to the hospital in a hurry. Bless the doctors and the nurses so they know what to do when the ambulance gets there. If there are people crying, make them feel a little better. Help them remember to pray to you so that pretty soon everything will be all right again. Amen.

I CAN PRAY FOR MYSELF!

My Prayer for Help From Jesus

JESUS, I want to be a good (boy, girl), but sometimes it is not easy for little kids like me to be good. Sometimes it isn't easy for anybody to be good—not all the time anyway. We need you to help us. We are like some toys that need a battery to make them do what they are supposed to do. You are not a battery, Jesus, but we need you to help us do what we are supposed to do. Help me, Jesus, so I will be as good as I can be. Amen.

My Prayer About My New Tooth

JESUS, I'm getting a new tooth. I can feel it with my tongue. I think you are very smart, Jesus, the way you let new teeth grow in our mouths and come in next to each other just like they are supposed to. I will take care of my teeth because I don't want to lose them. I think it would be hard to eat apples if I didn't have any teeth. Thank you, Jesus, for all my teeth. Amen.

My Prayer About Being Sick

JESUS, I feel sick today. I might have to take some medicine. I wish you would make me feel better so I don't have to take medicine. I don't like how it tastes. But I won't fuss about it. Thank you, Jesus, for how my mother (father, or other) takes care of me when I am sick. I wish you would help me and all the other sick people get well again. Amen.

My Prayer About How I Can Please Mommy

JESUS, I know some things Mommy likes me to do. She likes me to put away my toys after I finish playing so nobody stumbles over them. She likes it when I clean the dirt off my shoes before I come into the house so I won't mess up the carpet. She likes for me not to pile a lot of stuff on my plate and then not eat it. Jesus, help me today to do what makes Mommy happy. Let me do it to please you, too. I love you, Jesus. I love my mommy, too. Amen.

My Prayer About Sharing

JESUS, I like pie and cake and ice cream and and good things like that. Sometimes when I get to the table, I look for the biggest piece of pie or cake or the biggest dish of ice cream. I pick it up and put it by my place before anybody else gets it. Sometimes Daddy or Mommy makes me put it back. They say everybody should take turns sharing the good things. They say that somebody who always grabs the best things is selfish. Being selfish is not good. I don't want to be selfish. Please help me to share with others and not be selfish, Jesus. Amen.

My Prayer When Company Comes

JESUS, when company comes to our house and brings kids along, help me remember not to get rowdy with the kids and tear around in the house where we might break something. Help us have fun but not make Mommy have to fuss at me when the company goes home. Bless all our company and their kids. Amen.

My Prayer About Not Fussing

JESUS, sometimes Mommy or Daddy says, "Turn off the TV" or "It's time for you to go to bed" or "Wash your hands before you come to the table." And sometimes I fuss when they tell me things like that. I don't think you like for me to fuss about the things Mommy and Daddy tell me to do. Help me to do what I am told. Jesus, I think maybe you didn't always like it when your mother Mary or Saint Joseph told you to do some thing. But you did them anyway. I know you did, and I want to be like you. Amen.

My Prayer When I Need Somebody to Love Me

JESUS, most of the time I feel real good inside. But sometimes I don't, like when somebody won't listen when I talk or when nobody has time for me or maybe I did something I shouldn't have done but am sorry. I feel all by myself then. I keep wishing for somebody to love me.

I know you love me, Jesus. But sometimes I need Mommy or Daddy or somebody else to come and hug me and love me and tell me I am a good (boy, girl). When someone does that, it is like I come all alive again. Thank you, Jesus, for when people love me. I am glad you love me, too. Amen.

I CAN PRAY ABOUT GOD'S WORLD!

My Prayer About Going to the Supermarket

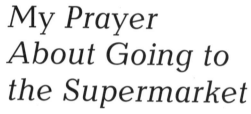

JESUS, sometimes I go to the supermarket with Mommy or Daddy. It's fun to go into the big store and look at everything. Sometimes when I see something I like—maybe candy or cookies—I ask Mommy or Daddy to buy it for me. If Mommy or Daddy think that what I ask for is something that is good for me, maybe they will buy it for me. But if Mommy or Daddy says no, they don't like for me to keep on asking right there in the store. They say that's acting like a baby. Jesus, help me not to act like a baby when I don't get what I want. Amen.

My Prayer About Trees

JESUS, I am glad you thought of making trees. They are cool to lie under when it's hot outside. I think the birds like trees, too, because they sit in them and sing. Trees are good to climb—but not too high or you might fall and hurt yourself. Lots of good things grow on trees, like oranges and apples and nuts. Sometimes people put a swing on a great big tree so kids can have fun. I wouldn't like it if there weren't any trees. Thank you, Jesus, for all the trees. Amen.

My Prayer About What Grows in the Ground

JESUS, a lot of things we eat, like carrots and radishes and potatoes, grow inside the ground. But when we cut these things open and look inside, the potatoes are clean inside, and the carrots are clean, and the radishes are clean inside, too. I think it is funny how they can be down in the dirt and not get dirty inside. Thank you, Jesus, for knowing how to let the things grow in the ground and not get dirty inside. Amen.

My Prayer About the Birds

JESUS, I think it is funny about the birds—how they fly. They just stand on the ground or on the fence and stretch out their wings, and right away they are flying. It must not be very hard to know how to fly because even little birds learn how to do it. I think it would be nice if people could fly like birds. Only we can't do it because we don't have wings. The birds need wings because if a cat comes after them, the birds can't run as fast as the cat. Jesus, I thank you for how the birds can fly to get away from cats. Amen.

My Prayer About a Closed-Up Flower

JESUS, I want to talk to you today about how when the flowers start to grow, they are closed up and look like little green balls on top of a stick. But when the balls open and the flowers come out, the flowers aren't a bit wrinkled or messed up. How a flower can be so tight inside that little ball and then come out so pretty—I don't know. Jesus, I think it is wonderful how you do that with the flowers. Amen.

My Prayer About Popcorn

JESUS, popcorn is a fun thing. It isn't at all like beans and peas and things like that. When you put beans or peas in a pan and make them hot, they keep on being beans or peas. But when you put popcorn in a pan and make it hot, the popcorn blows up big and white and puffy. If you put some salt and butter on the popcorn, it tastes even two times as good. Jesus, thank you for the way popcorn blows up and for how it is fun to eat. Amen.

My Prayer About How My Fingers Feel Things

JESUS, when I close my eyes and reach out and touch somebody's hair, I know it is somebody's hair, because it feels that way. If I keep my eyes closed and touch a cup, I know it is a cup and how it has a handle. And if I touch an apple or an orange or something else, I know what it is even if I don't look at it. Jesus, I think it is wonderful how our fingers are like that, because some people's eyes don't work the way they should, and they can't see anything. But if these people use their fingers, it's like they can see. Thank you, Jesus, for how our fingers can be almost like eyes sometimes. Amen.

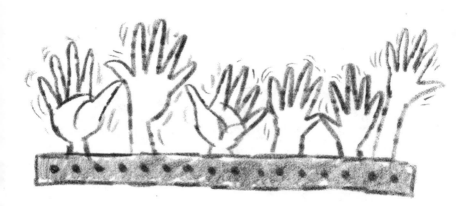

My Prayer About the Stars

JESUS, sometimes I am outside when it is dark, and I see a lot of stars in the sky. There are so many that I can't even count them. But I am glad for them. The sky would look so dark and empty if the stars went away. Jesus, you must be a very beautiful God to think of making so many beautiful things. I thank you for the stars. And I thank you that I have eyes to see them. Amen.

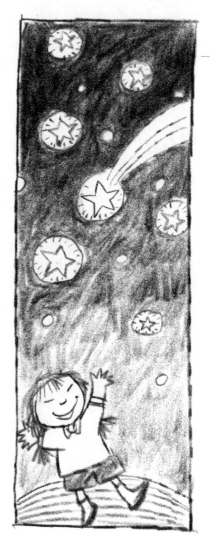

My Prayer About the Moon

JESUS, I like the moon. I like the way it gets big and then gets little and then goes away. It's different from the sun. The sun just stays big and round all the time. That's good. It would cause a lot of trouble if the sun got little on some days and then went away for some days. Kids would not like to go to school in the dark. If somebody batted a ball at recess time, it would be hard to find the ball if there was no light from the sun. I think the moon is best for nighttime, though, because it is easier to sleep if the sun is not shining in your eyes. Amen.

I CAN PRAY TO JESUS AND MARY!

My Prayer to Jesus' Mommy

JESUS, thank you for giving me your mommy to be my Mother Mary, too. I am glad for her to be my mother. That gives me two mommies. I love her very much. I know she watches over me and takes care of me, because that is what my mommy does.

Holy Mother Mary, thank you for letting all of us be your children. It's like you have an awfully big family, isn't it? Thank you for taking care of us. I love you, and when I get to heaven, I will be glad to see how beautiful you are. Amen.

My Prayer to Jesus in My Heart Room

JESUS, I know you are in my heart. It is like there is a little room inside my heart and you wait there all the time for me to come and talk with you. If I close my eyes and get real still, I can go into my heart room and find you there. Jesus, I want to go into my heart room now.

(Close your eyes and think that you open the door of your heart and walk right over to Jesus. See how happy he is to see you. Walk up close to Jesus, and let him put his arms around you. Tell him how much you love him. Then be very still and listen to what he might want to say to you. Tell Jesus you will come back into your heart room again and talk with him. Open your eyes now.)

Thank you, Jesus, for how I can go into my heart room whenever I want to and how I will always find you there waiting for me. I love you, Jesus. Amen.